KINGDOM COMMERCE

Seeing finances with an apostolic and prophetic eye

Also by Nicholas Dlamini

Five Senses Of Successful Leaders
How To Operate In Secular Babylon
The Apostolic And Prophetic Prayer Manual
There's A Serpent in my Way
Kingdom Commerce
Kingdom Commerce
Zion People

Table of Contents

Nicholas Dlamini

KINGDOM COMMERCE

First edition, 2024

Published by:

ND Publishers

Bethany, ESwatini

DEDICATION

I believe strongly in generational wealth. I believe that our predecessors failed to build generational wealth for us, hence we were born into poverty. There is nothing as difficult as being the first in your generation to do something great. The other day I told my brother, joking that since he was the first male in my father's house to get married, he will face all the demons for us who must follow.

This is an undeniable truth, that breaking through is the hardest when you are the first to do it in your bloodline. Both riches and poverty begin as an attitude, they then become a way of life, then after a while they become a reality. However, in the next generation they become a disposition.

I first dedicate this manuscript to my two children, Zipho and Jedidah. I pray that you won't have to face the same demons we had to face or make the same mistakes we made. Always know that you are always on my mind even though we are worlds apart because of life's predicaments.

Secondly, I would love to dedicate this work to my family, the Dlamini and the Mthembu clans. Many of you can relate to the struggle we faced fighting against poverty, trying to stay afloat. May this book become a tool to help you to come out of that struggle and have the life you always desired.

Lastly, I dedicate this book to the Body of Christ, especially to Black Africans and the Diaspora. All I can say is, this is our time. The African child is rising, and we need all the tools necessary for our rising. Do not miss this season. Do not miss what God is doing to set Africa free economically. I have published two books prior to this one, titled, Five

Senses Of Successful Leaders and How To Operate In Secular Babylon. This book is a sequel to both books and the main purpose for all three is to empower Africans that have been victims of systemic poverty to rise above all that.

ACKNOWLEDGEMENTS

There is a woman from Kanana, Hammanskraal named Lizzy that I want to appreciate. When I was in Bible College I was at my lowest; she took me in and served me. She practically became a mother to me. I never lacked because she was there. I want to acknowledge her input. Today my dreams have come true because of people like her.

It is people like her and others whom God used to get me to where I am today. I am forever grateful.

PREFACE

In this case study, we will look at finances. The principles written here are revelations the Lord gave me throughout the years. Some of these things I am still learning to walk in.

When reading a book or listening to a teaching, you will notice that it might be the same subject, but the level of revelation is likely to differ because of the maturity of the teachers or the Kairos they speak out of. Therefore, you might have heard a teaching on financial breakthrough under an old wineskin; if you haven't heard it under a new wineskin, your depth might not be the same as that of a new wineskin person.

We serve the same God who never changes; however, He changes the seasons and wineskins from time to time. Sometimes He allows the former to be destroyed to usher in the latter. There was once a time when the Jews and Samaritans were inaccurate on matters of worship. These people acknowledged the places of worship as founded by their patriarchs and prophets of old. When a new season came in, both views were erroneous. We do not want to find ourselves in error because we missed God. If you are familiar with this wineskin, then this book will be a confirmation.

"Kingdom Commerce" deals with how believers can rule in this world as kings and priests even around finances. I am persuaded by the notion that God desires for us to prosper. Prosperity is not a foreign concept; it is as scriptural as the rest of the premises found in the scriptures such as what the Word says about sufferings.

This book seeks to encourage believers on how they can overcome in the area of finances in the kingdom of as well as outlining the kingdom principles for how believers can prosper financially.

CHAPTER 1

INTRODUCTION TO KINGDOM COMMERCE

Imagine a situation where you have done everything physically and logically possible to prosper in life but for some reason nothing seems to happen for you. You have gone to school, you studied diligently, you obeyed your elders, you followed the rules, and most of all you are a good Christian person.

You have prayed when they told you to pray, you have paid your tithes when they told you to, and you even fasted, yet nothing is happening for you. You wonder what you are missing, what you are doing wrong. Is God picking on you? Why does it seem like others are prospering yet you do so much, and nothing happens? Do they perhaps know something you don't know?

Or imagine serving God faithfully and trusting Him and then your child gets sick, and your family wants you to take that child to a traditional healer. Other pastors have already prayed for your child and the doctors are unable to help. After doing all you know and spending all your money on physicians and going up and down to pastors/prophets what do you do?

Do you refuse for your family to take your children to the mediums? All this is hypothetical, however, there are many Christians that are faced with similar situations, where it seems that what they know works, scripturally, doesn't seem to work realistically. A plethora of believers are faithful when it comes to giving tithes and offerings, yet they struggle. Some pray and fast, yet they struggle. What are they doing wrong?

On the theological side of things, we can say, "many are the afflictions of the righteous" and forget to say, "but the Lord delivers him out of the ALL". NOTE the key word, viz. ALL. Even if we could argue that God allows us to go through some things for reasons sometimes known only by Him, we cannot deny that most believers go through things without answers, not because of the abovementioned reason.

The truth of the matter is, many people who struggle especially financially do so because they lack the proper apostolic and prophetic empowerment necessary to lift them up out of that situation, not because

God is somehow chastising them. I think most of us use this line of thought because we lack the proper diagnoses and prognoses for our current situations. Therefore, we blindly follow the logic that God knows and one day He will make us understand.

The theology of longsuffering has some colonial connotations to it. Don't get me wrong, longsuffering is scriptural, and it is a fruit of the Spirit, however, we cannot remain the victims of the system/matrix in the name of endurance. Biblical patience has a healthy context and should not be used to target a certain people group.

Black people in Africa and the Diaspora have been told to forgive in the name of the Bible to avoid any war or anarchy. However, this contextualized version of forgiveness is the reason why there are no reparations, and the black child remains economically bound. We will always be slaves as long as the white man benefits from the atrocities committed on the black man in the past.

I am not a political leader; I do not represent the interests of my people on a political platform. I am a prophet, I come with a word from the Lord, a prophetic blueprint that will not just cause a major wealth transfer in the church but also in the African continent and the Diaspora.

I believe in the prophetic and apostolic empowerment of God's people of all races and colors and like the apostle Paul my heart goes out to my very people of Africa and the dispersion. I write this book as a prophetic tool to help you level the scales of power without picking up a gun to fight. Prophetic people are still the most dangerous people on earth. As we study the prophetic people of old, we come to realize how powerful we are as the people of God. Once we come to understand the tools we have at our disposal, no systemic disadvantage can stop us.

My job as an apostolic and prophetic scribe is to help believers to recognize what we carry as the Body of Christ. Prophetic intelligence is a real thing. Remember what I asked you to imagine? Sometimes when things like that happen you get confused and wonder what you did wrong but out of the worse experiences you go through as a believer comes the best prophetic solutions you wouldn't know were possible had you not suffered first.

Whenever it seems like the heavens are closed against you and all you know seems to be failing there is a chance that you are a deliverer of your generation. There is something prophetic you are supposed to learn to deliver your generation. It's not that God does not want to deliver you, but He wants to teach you new prophetic intelligences that will help your generation. When what you know seems not to be working, God is getting ready to teach you what you do not know. It does not mean you should go to mediums, but it means that you should seek prophetic revelation.

THE APOSTOLIC AND PROPHETIC PERSPECTIVE

In all my theological writings I incorporate an apostolic and prophetic way of reasoning. The apostolic carters for the Biblical, theological foundation so that everything is in line with the scriptures and does not deviate from New Testament/Apostolic doctrine.

The prophetic carters for the proceeding revelations that flow from the throne of the Father generationally. Even though the apostolic revelation may remain the same the prophetic evolves while submitting to the restrictions and rules of the apostolic. The apostolic and prophetic should not be at odds with each other. They are two sides of the same coin.

While the apostolic is scriptural the prophetic is experiential. While the apostolic makes Biblical sense the prophetic makes sure believers have the Biblical experience. The apostolic forms a caucus but the prophetic acts. The apostolic deals with canonical, orthodox matters of God's truth and the prophetic deals with the somewhat cultic, unconventional keys with and without the scriptures.

The keys the prophetic provides might be frowned upon in the apostolic. Hence, leaders and believers need to be well versed with both the apostolic and prophetic, the Word and Spirit. Although the Spirit can never go against the Word, but He can go against one's understanding of the Word, thus causing the Apostolic believer to reject the prophetic, thinking, it is not from the Spirit of God.

Something may not be mentioned in the scripture, but it does not mean it is unscriptural. There is a difference between something that is mentioned in the Bible and something that is Biblical. E.g., genocide and slavery are mentioned in the scriptures, but it does not mean they are Biblical.

Another controversial subject is that of women preachers or pastors. If all we had was the Apostolic, we would reject every female person who attempts to preach or teach. Some will even go as far as saying they accept a woman's teaching as long as it is not within the walls of a church. That is even crazier, because if there are men within the audience then the woman should not teach men or exercise authority over them.

If we argued using only that lens, without the Holy Spirit then we would have hindered many women whom God has anointed. The prophetic helps us to recognize the Spirit even in difficult situations such as the abovementioned one. How does God anoint a woman and call her to pastoral ministry after He explicitly said she shouldn't be a pastor? I speak as a fool.

The key to breakthrough is found in the prophetic. Yes, sometimes, because of different theological conclusions one might reject a prophetic key, but I have learned that when God answers He answers through the prophetic. One's theological knowledge can hinder them from being flexible when they are Spirit-led to do something that they are not familiar with.

The good news is this is not new. We see how Ezekiel struggled when God told him to use human feces as a prophetic action. In a trance the apostle Peter struggled when God told him to kill unclean meat and eat. This was about to expose his faulty theology about the Gentiles. Our theology can be full of the traditions of men so much that it hinders the prophetic word of the Spirit.

On the other hand, a faulty theology can result to a false prophetic experience. Therefore, the doctrine helps us to recognize the move of the Spirit. In the book of Acts 13 the scripture tells us that there were teachers and prophets when the Holy Spirit spoke. A healthy prophetic gathering must have both teachers and prophets. The teaching mantle helps us to be Biblically sound and the prophetic mantle helps us to be spiritually sensitive. It is that sensitivity that releases practical keys for everyday living.

For example, your success is also connected to the place you live in. Sometimes the Holy Spirit can lead you to leave a certain place or country for you to have real success. The ground is somehow prophetically connected to your prosperity. Prophetically speaking you cannot prosper anywhere in the world. You can only prosper where the Holy Spirit says you can.

In the prophetic there are seasons, levels, strategies and doors/keys. All these have rules that are not necessarily prescribed in the scriptures (not to say they are unscriptural).

To want everything to be mentioned in the Bible for you to endorse it is also a sign of immaturity and bigotry. E.g., the word "trinity" is not in the Bible. The fact that there are three Persons of the Godhead and that these three are one is clearly demonstrated in the Bible. A foolish person argues based on where the word "trinity" is mentioned in the scriptures.

There are things which are clearly not mentioned in scripture that are scriptural. E.g., smoking is not mentioned to be a sin nor is doing drugs. Do we now go ahead, and smoke weed and do drugs because it is not mentioned in scripture? God forbid! How do we know it is a sin then? We know by the Spirit.

By the same Spirit we know that homosexuality is a sin even though a gay theologian can argue those verses and twist them around. We also know by the Spirit that Jesus died and rose again even though an atheist scholar might disagree. There are a lot of things that we know by the Spirit that are not written in the Word.

In the same way we can know by the Spirit which land had oil underneath, which deal will make us millions, and which country is the best to live in. The Spirit can tell you to buy a piece of land out of the blue not knowing that this land is a strategic position for your next enterprise and will make you millions.

Here is my attitude in life: if the Holy Spirit tells me to pursue something or someone I will pray and fast for as long as the Lord tells me that this thing or someone is a big part of my destiny. Once the Spirit says that this thing or person is no longer significant for what is to come, maybe because of a change in seasons I will forsake the pursuit.

This has helped me in knowing that no matter who or what I lose in life as long as I have the Holy Spirit, I can receive better things from Him. That is what I seek to instill in all my readers- the ability to become apostolic and prophetic. Don't just see things with an apostolic lens but also with a prophetic one.

The kingdom of God runs on its own economic principles.

Rom 12:2 says, *"And do not be conformed to this world, but be transformed by the renewing of your mind, that you may prove what is that good and acceptable and perfect will of God."*

The kingdom of God is not an imaginary kingdom; it is real. It has a real King and real subjects. God's kingdom has a real domain or realm, and that realm is spiritual and not physical. This should be the first thing one must learn about our kingdom- that is not earthly but heavenly. There is nothing earthly about it.

Understanding this will help us to understand the modus operandi of the kingdom and learn to work its system. One thing I've learned as a young black man is that success in the governments of the world is systematic. Knowing how to work the system puts you in a fighting position even though the system is rigged.

Another advantage in understanding kingdom finances is that it saves you from the systematic oppression in the world against certain people groups. The kingdom of God gives all people a fighting chance.

You must understand that even though God's kingdom is spiritual it affects the physical realm around that. One can even say that the spiritual kingdom is our currency because even when the banks refuse us, we still buy through applying kingdom principles.

The abovementioned scripture verse admonishes us not to conform to the operational dynamics of this world. Remember, I said the world systems are rigged against the working man. The economics of the world are designed to systematically oppress you, so that you remain slaves of the realm. Knowing how to work kingdom principles allows you the chance to arise amidst all the poverty and oppression.

It is incumbent, therefore, not to allow the patterns of this world to control you. As a believer you must learn how to think kingdom so that you can implement the kingdom way in a worldly environment. If the kingdom is spiritual, then its principles are spiritual. If the principles of the kingdom are spiritual, then they are most likely to contradict the natural or carnal way of doing things.

The believer must learn and understand the spiritual kingdom and the spiritual principles that run it to be able to draw its eternal power. The good thing about the kingdom is that its power can be transferred to anything we need physically be it healing, counsel, peace, or money. Yes, you heard me; I said, money.

As a follower of Jesus Christ one of the things you need to master is how to import goods from heaven to earth. When dealing with the business of buying things overseas one must also understand foreign exchange and shipping. If you travel to other countries and buy goods, you must also understand how those goods are declared and how customs work.

All those are dynamics one must learn if one desires to do business internationally. The same is true with the kingdom of God. There is earth's economy and there's heaven economy. Learning earthly economics is not enough, you must also learn heavenly economics.

For the average human, the possibility is they are not successful because they don't understand the political and economic system of their country. In other words, they don't know how to milk the systemic cow that has all the money they need. However, for us as kingdom people it is not just about knowing how to milk the political and economic cow of your country.

You can become a billionaire without milking those cows. Through the spirit of revelation, I am convinced that it is possible to be rich without falling into the spirit of shadiness that we see in the world.

The kingdom's system is not like earthly economic systems; it is not rigged against you. It is designed for you to make it. No matter where you are in the world you can apply kingdom principles and prophetic keys and make it. So, maybe you never finished school, or you come from a poor background; it really doesn't matter. The promises of God are for you too.

CHAPTER 2

UNDERSTANDING KINGDOM CURRENCIES

When you are working with finances you will be introduced to currencies. What is a currency? According to Merriam Webster, currency is what goes in circulation as a medium of exchange and is legally and customarily used as a measure of value, or a means of payment.

In the present world, money is understood to be a currency. Money is either a piece of paper or coined that is legally approved for the purposes of buying and selling. Money by itself, especially paper money, is not valuable but what makes it valuable it what it represents, e.g., minerals, such as gold, copper etc.

Every country has a currency of its own. These currencies are not equal in value and therefore do not have the same buying power. Some have stronger buying power than others. E.g., the South African rand is stronger than the Zim dollar yet when compared to the American dollar the rand is significantly low.

The irony here is, the country with most minerals, named, Zimbabwe has the lowest currency and the countries without minerals such as European countries and the United States have the highest currencies. How is that possible? It is because they have rigged the game for their own political gain and it's working.

Now, in the kingdom of God there is a medium of exchange, a currency called "faith" (Heb 11:1).

In our kingdom there is nothing you can receive without faith. First, economically speaking, we do business in the kingdom through giving and receiving and not buying and selling. Buying and selling as a Babylonian or secular system. We use it because we live in the world, but it is not how we prosper.

Therefore, just as money is the currency that is used in worldly business or transactions, faith is the currency that we use in kingdom business. In the kingdom, anything you get is possible through faith. Even if you're involved in business, that business cannot prosper unless you have a heavenly currency.

Therefore, God's currency is universal. It works in all the realms for the benefit of His children. However, a currency is nothing but paper unless it is backed up by resources that strengthen it. The same is true with faith. Hence, this chapter is dubbed "kingdom currencies"; these are the virtues that give you buying power in the kingdom of God.

2Pe 1:5-7 But also for this very reason, giving all diligence, add to your faith virtue, to virtue knowledge, 6 to knowledge self-control, to self-control perseverance, to perseverance godliness, 7 to godliness brotherly kindness, and to brotherly kindness love.

Now, if you look at the abovementioned faith supplements you will realize that these are like Paul's fruit of the Spirit. Let's view them.

Gal 5:22, 23 But the fruit of the Spirit is love, joy, peace, longsuffering, kindness, goodness, faithfulness, gentleness, self-control. Against such there is no law.

If you take every virtue counted in the New Testament, including the book of Colossians I believe we have more than nine fruit of the Spirit. These are the minerals that strengthen the currency of the kingdom. Without this one's faith cannot produce the necessary results.

Galatians calls them "the fruit of the Spirit" as if to shift the responsibility of production to the Holy Ghost but Peter seems to emphasize that it takes the diligence of the believer to add to their faith all these supplements. It is our responsibility to make sure that we see results in the kingdom.

Hence, Peter continues to say, "Therefore, brethren, be even more diligent to make your call and election sure, for if you do these things you will never stumble" (2 Pet 1.10). So, the fruit of the Spirit are the things we must diligently pursue with the help of the Holy Spirit. In most cases when results are lacking it is not because of a lack of faith but a lack of kingdom minerals that make our faith to work.

Look at what Paul says in Galatians 5:6, "For in Christ Jesus neither circumcision nor uncircumcision avails anything, but faith working through love." The love makes the faith to work properly. We as black people in Africa and the diaspora have never struggled with faith. We are a theistic people. Therefore, when our faith towards God is not working it must because it is weak or little. What makes faith weak or little is when we lack the necessary ingredients that make faith to work.

So what are these kingdom currencies? Here I have listed only five currencies beginning with faith.

Faith. The main medium of exchange.

Hope. The deep expectation of God's intervention.

Love. For God and people.

Knowledge. You can't believe what you are not exposed to through knowledge.

Godliness. The fear of the Lord or obedience.

There are more currencies such as holiness, gentleness, humility etc.

As already stated, the other currencies are simply ingredients that make faith to work. Begin to add to your faith and get the desired results.

CHAPTER 3

APOSTOLIC STRATEGIES FOR FINANCIAL BREAKTHROUGH

When we read the book of Revelations thirteen, we learn of what I call Mammon - the commercial anti-Christ. Of course, the scripture is clear about the fact that there's an idol, a Baal, that runs the commercial world called Mammon.

This Mammon is also dubbed Babylon the Great by John. In Revelations 13, we see two beasts: one emerging from the sea and the other from the ground. I call the first beast Babylon or Mammon, a carnal beast that seeks to be worshipped or recognized. The second beast, I call death (see chapter 8). For people to operate in the realm of the first beast, Babylon, they must receive a mark on their foreheads and right hands from the second beast.

Let me use another example, friends: the two beasts speak of two realms. The first beast is the physical realm in all its departments, economics, politics etc. Please remember that the first beast with seven heads symbolizes Rome with seven mountains, but I am using this analogy to illustrate a point. Seven pagan nations were supposed to be conquered by the Jews in Canaan (Deut 7:1). There are seven sectors in the secular world; let us say these represent the seven heads of the beast, Mammon.

The success of businesspeople and politicians doesn't depend on the first beast (i.e., money). It depends on the second beast, Death. Now this issue about beasts and marks is not new or scary because we also have a Beast, the Lion of the tribe of Judah, the Lamb of God. This Beast is life. While Babylon's beast represents death, our Beast is Life. The success of every businessperson or politician depends on a certain beast. We call this the occult.

Read Revelation 13:16-18

666 is a very crucial number in both commerce and politics. No successful politician doesn't have this number on their forehead or right hand. The tattoo is completely spiritual. The forehead and the right hand are symbolic just as the beasts are. Now can you imagine a businessperson

without a proper relationship with Christ? Such a person cannot operate in secular Babylon without the triple six.

We who serve the one true Beast have also received a mark on our right hands and foreheads. The number is 777. It is the number of God, the number of His name. Once our businesspeople, politicians, and musicians have been fully baptized in the name of the Father, the Son, and the Holy Spirit, Mammon will bow, and gold will be restored to God's people.

It's amazing how the mark must be put on the right hand, not the left hand! Benjamin is 'son of my right hand.' We cannot raise financial giants who are spiritual grasshoppers. Remember the saying by bishop Jakes, "Grasshoppers don't eat grapes"?

All financial giants you know who do not serve God went to serious occultic lengths to get where they are today. All buyers and sellers have a mark of a beast. Whose mark do you have? What is the spiritual secret of your success?

Read Genesis 14:21

666 is the number of enterprises. It is the number of buying and selling. Those who embark in business without Christ have the mark of the beast or are influenced by it. The mark is currently entering the church stronger than before. It is a number that emphasizes the number of "goods" one has more than the number of souls. The term "goods" is one letter from the term "gods."

"And the **prince of darkness** said to Abram, give me the **souls**, and take the **gods** to yourself."

This is very evident in the church today. We teach that faith is like money, i.e., a medium of exchange. So, people get into the Word because they believe that their car or house is in it. With faith, they can buy what they need. They don't buy; they claim because Christ's blood has done the transactions. As true as this might be, the focus has shifted from the Great Commission to a money scheme.

WHY DO WE NEED FINANCIAL BREAKTHROUGHS?

Let us revisit why we need the left hand in the church. The greatest misconception in the church is our perception of heaven. Many believers can't wait to get out of their hard lives to get to heaven, gold crowns, and walk on gold streets. Now think about it, what is the use of me following Christ if I'm following Him for an earthly price? What use is gold to me in heaven? Think about it.

The second misconception is our doctrine on the blessing of Abraham. We have created this materialistic view of the blessing promised to Abraham. Let us look at whether the blessing promised to Abraham is materialistic or spiritual.

Read Genesis 12:1-3

Was God referring to money when he said, "I will bless you"? No friend, that already Abraham was a rich man.

Read Gen 13:2

The Lord did not need to speak of money because Abraham had money. Look at the blessing promised to him in chapter twelve; it consisted of the nations. The name "Abram" means "exalted father," but God changed his name to Abraham, which means "a father of many." God refers to two realms when promising Abraham sons. He speaks of the sand of the sea, a type of the natural and then He speaks of the stars of heaven, a type of the spiritual.

We know that the natural comes first and then the spiritual. God promises two covenants: one carries an earthly lineage and a heavenly one. One is according to the Law, and another is according to grace. God demonstrates this when He gives Abraham a son through a slave woman who is a type of the nation of Israel. Then, Isaac is born of a free woman who is a type of the church under grace.

I always wonder why believers sing "Abraham's blessings are mine" every time they give offerings and tithes. They should sing that when they receive the Holy Ghost. They should say, "Abraham's blessing is mine," not, "Abraham's blessings are mine." The scripture says: "Christ has redeemed us from the curse of the law, having become a curse for us (for it is written, cursed is everyone who hangs on a tree that the blessing of Abraham might come upon the Gentiles in Christ Jesus, that we might receive the promise of the Spirit through faith." (Gal 3:13-14).

The question is, how can Abraham bestow upon the Gentiles that he did not receive? The answer must be that he can't. The question must arise again if Abraham can pass down the Holy Ghost generationally, when and how did he receive Him (the Spirit)? In simple terms, was Abraham filled with the Holy Ghost?

"And Melchizedek king of Salem brought forth bread and wine: and he *was* the priest of the most high God. And he blessed him, and said, Blessed *be* Abram of the most high God, possessor of heaven and earth: And blessed be the most high God, which hath delivered thine enemies into thy hand. And he gave him tithes of all" (Gen 14:18-20 KJV).

It is evident in this text that the Holy Ghost is sending us clues about the actual transference of the blessing which God promised to Abraham in Genesis 12. Remember, Abraham could not bear a son until he received the power of the Holy Spirit, who quickened his mortal body. Abraham received the Holy Ghost, and in Isaac, he laughed. Prophetically speaking, Isaac is a child of the Holy Ghost. The Spirit quickens our mortal bodies also when we receive Him.

Another piece of evidence is in the two ministries found only in Melchizedek. These ministries were now evident in the Israeli nation, which was a royal priesthood. The same ministries are transferred onto us when we receive the Holy Ghost.

All this is evidence that money is not the blessing promised to Abraham. To know this is liberating to the soul. It helps us to pray for finances for the right reasons, viz., for establishing God's kingdom and advancing its message on earth.

Read Exodus 25:1-9

The greatest purpose for accumulating wealth is building the Lord's tabernacle on earth.

Read Haggai 2:6-9

Why does the Lord bring the issue of money in the middle of such a prophecy? From chapter one, He's rebuking Israel about His house, viz., the Body of Christ. He says to the leaders who are church minded:

"Then came the word of the LORD by Haggai the prophet, saying, *Is it* time for you, O ye, to dwell in your ceiled houses, and this house *lie* waste? Now therefore thus saith the LORD of hosts; Consider your ways. Ye have sown much, and bring in little; ye eat, but ye have not enough; ye drink, but ye are not filled with drink; ye clothe you, but there is none warm; and he that earneth wages earneth wages *to put it* into a bag with holes. Thus saith the LORD of hosts; Consider your ways. Go up to the mountain, and bring wood, and build the house; and I will take pleasure in it, and I will be glorified, saith the LORD. Ye looked for much, and, lo, *it came* to little; and when ye brought *it* home, I did blow upon it. Why? saith the LORD of hosts. Because of mine house that *is* waste, and ye run every man unto his own house. Therefore the heaven over you is stayed from dew, and the earth is stayed *from* her fruit. And I called for a drought upon the land, and upon the mountains, and upon the corn, and upon the new wine, and upon the oil, and upon *that* which the ground bringeth forth, and upon men, and upon cattle, and upon all the labor of the hands" (Hag 1:3-11 KJV)

He speaks to those men of God who have not set their minds on the city church. In chapter two, He promises a shaking through His Word. But such shaking, who can sponsor it? The Lord Himself will bring finances to those whose hearts are right. This is what I call 777; a kingdom mind that focuses on financing the purposes of God.

CHAPTER 4

LEVELS OF FINANCIAL BREAKTHROUGH IN THE LOCAL CHURCH

There are five levels of financial breakthroughs in the local church. Tithes and offerings, employment, debt cancellation, entrepreneurship, and ownership. Let's take a closer look at these levels one by one.

Tithes and offerings

The first and foremost sign of a breakthrough in the local church is when believers give tithes and offerings without murmuring. I want to bring this insight to you, beloved: when you study the Abrahamic view of tithe, you can see that it was not a law but a way of honor. Abraham gave the tithe of the spoils to honor the prophet Melchizedek because he recognized grace upon him.

When grace is upon a man, it is easy to honor it through material things. Hence, the set man receives tithe in your local church, not necessarily God. Those who receive spiritual nourishment from their spiritual teacher must reciprocate by sharing material things with him. Tithe is a practical system of honoring the set-man. I speak pragmatically, not regarding theological debates.

Under the Law of Moses, tithe was a command and ritual; people paid tithe in the house of God. Before the Law, tithes were given, not paid, not out of a theological compulsion but as a seemingly random act that went from Abraham to his descendants. Was there a revelation behind this act? I believe so; however, there is no evidence for it being taught or required.

Some who protest the tithe claim that Abraham copied the act from pagan practices. This also is speculative. The most plausible inference is that Abraham received the tithing revelation from God as he did other practices, such as circumcision. It becomes clear that the patriarchs gave their tithes to do the following:

a. To honor God by giving to a prophet (i.e., Melchizedek)
b. As a form of worship
c. To acknowledge that it is God who gave you the power to

create wealth.
d. To take care of the sent ones of the Lord.
e. To entertain strangers (unknowingly, one might receive an
    angel).

Please understand that certain principles in the bible are rightly called universal laws because they control the universe. The law of sowing and reaping is universal, and so is the law of tithes and first fruits. It's not God's way of placing a curse upon you. Like I always say, in ZCC, they drink tea, but they don't call it tea. They call it "tayelo' meaning "an instruction." The same applies to tithe; it is an instruction from the Lord that works in us to activate the realm of finances so that we become spiritual principalities.

Now, is this a requirement/statute? No, it is not an eternity-based principle such as holiness. If you are not a tither, you are still a child of God. I believe you are missing out on the part of your life that would benefit you. However, your salvation is not affected by that. Let me give an example of fasting; you can live and not fast. Some teach against fasting in the New Testament; this is their prerogative, but it is unwise.

What are curses? They are mentalities that cause impurities that limit us. Tithing affects your mindset; it has a way of activating your faith dynamics through obedience. So, tithing helps you to help yourself, it teaches us how to live as kings by thinking as such. Why is it a curse not to tithe? It is because when your heart does not release the money, it enthrones it subconsciously. Once your heart follows money as an idol, it ceases to follow God, so the heavens get shut. The believer becomes a rich useless person. All sorts of devourers enter his life, including debts, bad habits, and bad luck. When you honor God with your money, your heart learns to trust the Lord and His salvation. In the day of trouble and crises, the Lord can remember you.

My words cannot express clearly and fully the importance of this. Some of the things I wish to say are not written in the scriptures, but

I received from the Lord that which I wish to deliver to you. Unfortunately, our forefathers saw in part, and they did not see some of the things we see today.

Adam's first act of worship and obedience in the garden regarded material things. The tree of knowledge of good and evil (not its name but its purpose on earth) was forbidden to men. Figuratively, this tree served as the first fruits of the entire garden. Good energy filled the garden if its fruits fell on the ground and rotted. One can even say that the tree was holy unto the Lord. Once Adam ate one fruit from the tree, doubt entered his heart, and he lost his position.

Oh, friend! The tithe deals with you. It transforms you from the natural sense to the supernatural sense. Think about it, Cain's heart was exposed for the witch that he was after God rejected his first fruits offering. Money exposed the evil in his heart. Also, Judas' heart was exposed after a woman gave expensive perfume to the Lord. To the pure, all things are pure.

"Do not eat the bread of a miser, nor desire his delicacies; for as he thinks in his heart, so is he. (Pro 23:6-7).

This is a serious test of the heart - a meal. Try receiving pledges from people who don't tithe and see if they'll fulfill their faith promise. How will they buy the whole sound system if they fail to bring 10% unto the Lord? How will a person tithe if he complains in his heart when he's supposed to give people food?

"For if the firstfruit is holy, the lump is also holy; and if the root is holy, so are the branches" (Rom 11:16).

Now notice that the apostle uses the word "first fruit" as an example, not a doctrine. He parallels that with the example of the root of a tree that if the root is holy, the fruit will obviously conform to the nature of its parent. In your finances, this principle works in the context of tithes.

My point here is that money is not holy on its own, but tithes are holy. If you decide to eat your first fruits, viz. tithes, you declare your finances as common. Holiness protects your money, and that dynamic is activated when you honor God with your first fruits. By so doing, you declare God as the owner and protector of your bank account. You see, beloved, anything can happen to your money. Crises will surely strike but let me assure you that if your money is God's money, then God will not allow the devil to steal His money.

There are three types of offerings in the Bible:

Free will offering. Exodus 25:2

The free will offering served as Moses' building fund. The people brought what their leader asked, emphasizing a willing heart. Free will is somewhat of a gift offering. It is called a gift in the New Testament and is greatly encouraged by Christ and the apostles.

Tithe or 10% Malachi 3:10

Tithes fall under the family of first things. Hence, the tithe is timeless because of the principle it represents. The tithe carries a weightier implication than free will. One of the reasons for this is that tithing is a relationship response, whereas giving is a heart desire.

I give because I am moved to give, I don't have to; I want to. I am not grateful for anything, but I am doing it out of the willingness of my heart. In all practicality, tithing is impossible without a relationship. I tithe because I recognize the grace that is working for me. I respond to my Melchizedek (for lack of a better word).

First fruits or 100%

Proverbs 3:9-10; Luke 21:1; Acts 4:32-37

The first fruits is more of a concept than it is an offering. It can translate to finances, but it is symbolic of how much one is willing to sacrifice for the kingdom. Tithe opens the windows (realms, ideas, dimensions) of heaven but the first fruits (or the willingness to lose or give away everything for the Gospel) enhance apostolic ministry through signs and wonders. This is also a clear indication of the power of receiving grace by way of giving. This, however, is the beginning of financial growth in the local church. It breaks down the stony heart of jealousy and stinginess so that a compassionate heart may emerge.

Another person may want to raise the issue of feeding the poor and why I am not mentioning it. Feeding the poor is part of the mandate of the church. When believers give in the house of God, one of the primary agendas is to feed the poor. The gospel we preach to the poor must be practical, not verbal, because most poor people reverence God more than the rich. Most of them pray more and know more about God than some greatest scholars.

If a believer wishes to feed the poor, he must consider the following:

1. We will always have the poor with us.
2. The poor are not number one in God's timeline, but the kingdom is.
3. One should not place poor people above the set man, like Judas, who got offended when the Set Man was honored.
4. People should not excuse themselves from supporting the church financially by claiming that they are feeding the poor.
5. One should start in the household of faith to give and take care of those in need.

(Gal 6:10).

Employment

There second level of financial breakthrough in the local church is employment. One of the greatest assets of the local church is divine favor. That favor is evident at the workplace, home, and job hunting. A supernatural power can be released through the local presbytery that can cause job hunters to become job hunted.

This is the second sign that the local church is breaking forth to her financial destiny. This level is very important, especially in rural areas where it's hard to run a ministry or business. A ministry can thrive in a village through the tithes and offerings from working believers coming home every weekend and at the end of the month.

Even if believers are willing to tithe and give, they cannot advance the church to its purposes if they are unemployed. When God visits the local church, financially, believers become employed, and others are promoted. According to the scriptures, this is to advance God's kingdom through giving. At first, the Lord breaks the spirit of stinginess and the spirit of unemployment.

JOB HUNTING

One of the greatest challenges in our localities is that our spiritual leaders do not empower our youth to be financially successful. They raise their followers to be ministry-centered instead of business-minded or work-minded. While it is true that God calls people into full-time ministry, in most cases the church doctrine plays a huge role in conditioning the people to lean towards becoming preachers rather than entrepreneurs.

People say, "Money can't buy happiness." This might be true morally, but pragmatically every time I had money, I had a wide smile. Why? Because I knew that my kids were covered and that I could take care of my family and those in need and fulfill my mandate quicker.

Bishop Noel Jones preached some years ago, saying it's a question of power. Yes, I agree. What power? Power to create wealth. Otherwise, what's the point in raising the dead if you cannot feed your family? Dear servant of God, you cannot afford to starve your family in the name of the calling; stop protecting the Lord. Go and work and put food on the table; Paul did it. Otherwise, you will be bitter in life or cheat your way into success. You will end up taking offerings at gunpoint.

Think about it for a minute: nobody called you, but God, and nobody feels what you are feeling but you. You must make it happen because, at the end of the day, nobody cares but you. Sadly, even your spiritual father might only be using you to advance his mission. Until you accept that it's you, God, and the people He brings your way, you will stumble before you make it. You will trust in men, and men will fail you. Therefore, work with your hands to finance your mandate here on earth.

Some people get offended when I say, "even your pastor probably doesn't care about you." Of course, I don't mean all pastors, but how many men of God do you know who seek souls for the sake of saving them? Very few. Today, if I start a church, it's another way of making money in most cases. Think about it: why do you think everybody is starting their ministry if we are working for the same King? At first, the answer would be "because of differences in vision and doctrine," but not today.

The reason is simple; every one for themselves. Even the apostolic move, which started with fire and innocence, has become more manipulative and controlling than Hebronic relationships. So, I forewarn and forearm all ministry virgins who think everybody is holy and just. Welcome to the Babylon of ministry, where apostles and bishops curse and assassinate anyone who rises in "their" cities. News flash: no one is out there to promote you. Therefore, empower yourself financially and do your thing and mind your own business. And if you find that one man of God who is pure, praise the Lord and don't let go. However, always bare this in mind:

"As it is written, There is none righteous, no, not one: There is none that understandeth, there is none that seeketh after God. They are all gone out of the way, they are together become unprofitable; there is none that doeth good, no, not one.Their throat *is* an open sepulchre; with their tongues they have used deceit; the poison of asps *is* under their lips: Whose mouth *is* full of cursing and bitterness: Their feet *are* swift to shed blood: Destruction and misery *are* in their ways: And the way of peace have they not known: There is no fear of God before their eyes" (Rom 3: 10-18 KJV).

It is with regret and sorrow of heart that I quote this verse as it applies more to today's leaders (and most definitely to me, who has sinned the most). May God help us! Those who know Babylon and cruelty in the ministry will agree with a loud Amen to what I am saying.

DECOLONIZING BIBLICAL SPIRITUALITY

What Africa needs now more than ever is economic freedom. Africans have been fed with an imperial view that exalts the suffering and patience of the African believers. This contextual theology of poverty and suffering has subconsciously caused Africans to frown upon any African or African preacher that prospers financially.

Don't get me wrong; there is a level of corruption and occult that people go through to make their millions; however, there is also the mentality that black success is demonic and white success is right. List any African billionaire or multimillionaire you think isn't involved in the occult. That should say a lot about the African mindset.

I love the Lord; I am not in any way cultic or shady; however, when the money comes in, I will be labeled among the charlatans; it is the way of the world. Not every rich African is evil; we need to decolonize even in our sermons. Africans need to be financially empowered. A poverty-centered gospel must fall. Because of this kind of mentality, some preachers end up overcorrecting in fear of being labeled by the world.

I will be unapologetically wealthy; my children and their children after them will be wealthy; the devil is a liar! I have tried poverty, and it doesn't feel good; small is not holy.

Debt cancelation

Freedom is one of the major human forces that motivate change. A man can do anything to gain his freedom. Even in the ministry, nothing fulfills a man of God more than to be free, especially financially. Freedom from debt is everybody's dream.

Having the money you need to get things done in your life is very fulfilling, especially if you have things to do with money, such as fulfilling your vision. Lack of money releases a certain level of slavery; hence, we have employers and employees. No one loves to be one's employee, but what can one do when they have bills to pay? We often say, "That's life." However, that isn't life. That is not the kind of life God wants for you.

Remember, friends; there is a difference between the kind of life God desires for you and God's kind of life. God's kind of life is Zoe, and I'll show you in the next few chapters what God's kind of life is. However, in this chapter, I'm showing you the kind of life God wants you to live as His child. I haven't come to divinity or sonship. As you can see, all our manuscripts are transitioning the children of God into their level of sonship.

One of the things that God desires for you is that you live a debt-free life. In other words, you should be a slave to the Word and nothing else. The Word of God shows us that it's possible to be debt-free.

Read Deuteronomy 28:1-12

We call this the blessing. You can see here that God was addressing prosperity on a national level. An entire government can be debt-free. A young preacher once asked, "does God bless you because you've done something, or does He simply bless you?" Of course, I did not answer him because I knew he was planning to do wrong. However, most people do not understand the difference between the goodness of the Lord and His blessing.

God is good to all people, giving them all sunshine and rain regardless of who they are and whether they serve Him. You could call that a blessing, but God is good. The blessing has to do with the Holy Spirit, and the New Testament condition of the blessing is faith. Not all have the blessing, but all see the goodness of the Lord.

The Old Testament condition for the blessing is works. As you can see in the above scripture, the demand is to do all that is commanded. However, in the New Covenant, the demand is to believe all that is written. The only common thing between covenants is hearkening to the voice of God. This was regarding the Law in the Old Covenant, but under the New Covenant, this is regarding faith. This means that the

Law must not be in tablets but written in your heart until you become the Law itself.

The blessing comes by faith, and it is spiritual. It gives us the power to create wealth. The wealth creation part is a choice, but we all possess the power to do so.

"The blessing of the LORD makes one rich, And He adds no sorrow with it" (Pro 10:22).

This means that the blessing makes it possible for you to be rich, but it does not drag you to riches without your participation of faith. I have to say these things because most believers are poor, and they blame God for it. I have done it. It's possible to be blessed and still live a life of sorrow. Please understand that the blessing is good in that it will make you rich, but it is not riches themselves. It is when you are rich that sorrow is dealt with. So just because I have the blessing does not mean I'll be happy if I'm broke. Many believers do not take advantage of the blessing.

Debt cancelation is not only a promise, but it is a command. Paul says, "Owe no one anything except to love one another, for he who loves another has fulfilled the law" (Rom 13:8).

The Lord would not command it if it were impossible to live debt-free. In this subject, I want to cover the supernatural way of debt cancelation, not the common way, because already many writers have taught how to come out of debt.

The question is, can a person supernaturally come out of debt and stay free from it? Yes, you can (Philippians 4:13; Mark 11:22-23).

The above scriptures are living proof that one can live debt-free. All things are possible to him who believes. There is a supernatural way of coming out of debt as well as the financial one. The financial one has three, seven or ten steps but the supernatural way is only one principle-the voice of God.

When you want to hear God's voice, you need to get into the Word and prayer to flush out of your spirit anything that can block your hearing. People look for many formulas, but there is none but one God and how you relate to Him. Hearing the voice of God will save you a lot of energy and money. This is the only way you can live financially free.

In the Old Testament, God used prophets, and He still uses them; however, in the new covenant, we have better promises; not only do we have prophets, but we can also hear God's voice for ourselves. Every born-again believer has the Holy Spirit, who guides them to all truth. Sons of God are not those who follow a prophet but those who follow the Holy Spirit.

Let me show you examples of people who obeyed the Holy Spirit and beat hunger and poverty by their obedience:

"Abram was very rich in livestock, in silver, and in gold" (Gen 13:2). This was after God called him out of Haran in chapter 12.

"And Elijah said to her, do not fear; go and do as you have said, but make me a small cake from it first, and bring it to me; and afterward make some for yourself and your son. For thus says the LORD God of Israel: The bin of flour shall not be used up, nor shall the jar of oil run dry, until the day the LORD sends rain on the earth" (1Ki 17:13-14).

Notice that in the above scriptures, there is nothing wise that these guys did except that they obeyed the voice of God. In the following scripture, you will see that common and supernatural senses are applied.

Read 2 Kings 4:1-7

The first part of the instruction is a supernatural sense all the way. However, when the miracle happened, the woman returned to the prophet, and he gave her a business idea. The stock was supernatural, but the woman had to sell to cancel her debt. At times God can supernaturally provide capital and then instruct you on what and how to sell.

I remember the other day in East London I needed money for transport to return home to KwaNdebele. I had R100 and God told me to saw a R50 seed, and when I did, I received R500. Sometimes God can command ravens to bring you meat but first you must believe that even ravens can feed you when God sends them.

Sometimes God can supernaturally take you out of debt without your participation. All He'll want is for you to believe. Let me show examples.

Read 2 Kings 6:1-7; 7:1-2

God can do things that can blow your mind if you just believe. Abraham did nothing special in the natural to receive Isaac, but he believed the word that spoke to Him. You can be a millionaire in one hour if God says so. Never be presumptuous but wait on God. Let your confidence be in God's voice, not your abilities. People are becoming occult because they fail to listen to the voice of God.

Read Psalm 103:20

When we accurately hear the voice of God, we unlock the ministry of angels. God's voice in us commands the angels on our behalf because we do God's will. Obeying God's Word puts us in authority even above angels.

Read James 1:22

Now, notice here that hearing precedes doing. You cannot do properly if you don't hear correctly. Prosperity begins when we take time to receive directions from the Holy Spirit. Even faith will rise when we listen to the voice of God. When the voice of God is rare in our lives, miracles become a thing of the past, and life becomes hard. The voice of God saved the Shunammite from an impending crisis, and the Bible says everything was restored to her seven times more than before. Now, under the new covenant, we are looking at 30, 60, and 100 times more.

Entrepreneurship

At this level, believers in the local church begin to venture into business. They start projects, own companies, and take risks. It is good to have working people, but it is more powerful to have entrepreneurs in the church. It is good to have people who sometimes close million-rand deals.

With the blessing of the Lord upon you, you are guaranteed two things: riches and no sorrow. We need wealth creators in the church, not just government employees. If you believe God that you'll be a multi-billionaire, then you cannot do that teaching at a primary school. Entrepreneurship is the only key to true riches. Even if you are exceptionally talented in something such as soccer, you cannot be like that forever; hence you need to invest your money. You need to embark on some enterprise.

Ownership

The next logical level of the prosperity of the local church is ownership. First, individuals will begin to own businesses, as I've already stated. Then they'll own shares, property, land etc. Then the church will begin to own land, farms, malls, hospitals, private schools etc.

Now, that can happen due to sponsors, but in this case, I'm talking about wealth. A wealthy church does not need sponsorship per ser. When a child grows, he does not need a support system because he can walk alone and sometimes feed himself. This applies more to the black church; we need to free ourselves from white saviors. We need to finance our visions.

CHAPTER 5

DIVINITY IN PROSPERITY

One of the most powerful cutting-edge truths of the 21st century is the apostle Vincent Kobane's famous statement on divinity: "the Word became flesh so that the flesh might become the Word." God's ultimate goal is Himself.

There are two Adams who represent two races. The first Adam is humanity and its nature, and the second Adam is the divine race (viz., The sons of God). The first Adamic nature is earthly, human, perishing, sinful, sick, undesirable, corruptible, and mortal. The second nature is divine, holy, immortal, unadulterated, and incorruptible.

With the fall of Adam came all the misfortunes mentioned above, and with the advent of the second Adam came eternal life. The kingdom of God revolves around this truth about the two Adams. These are the two beasts I mentioned earlier. The first beast is Anti-Christ, earthly, terminal, and passing away, and the second Beast is Christ, heavenly, life-giving, and eternal.

Now, I want you to realize that whatever nature a person carries becomes his title. For example, the church is entitled "Body of Christ" because it carries the nature of Christ through Holy Communion. It is also called Zion because it has come to Zion. The first Adam carries the nature of sin and death and is rightly called sin or death. The phrase, "He became sin for us," indicates that Adamically speaking, we were sin and not just sinful. Even now, we are not only righteous, but we are righteousness. By this, I conclude that the nature of a thing is its title.

"Jesus said to him, I am the way, the truth, and the life. No one comes to the Father except through Me" (Joh 14:6).

Notice that He says, "I am..." not, "I have." What He is loaded with is what He is titled by the Holy Spirit. Therefore, here is the order: Adam is death, and Christ is life. By simply understanding this order, we realize that there's no way on earth that Jesus died to save Adam and his children, but He died to replace Adam and His children. One way or another, God has been and is busy killing the first Adam.

Adam's condition is terminal and cannot be redeemed; hence, God behooved to send another Adam to replace the first. Jesus didn't die so that in you can exist a blood-washed old Adam, but He wants you all to Himself. He is not trying to improve you, but He's trying to replace you.

I speak in the dimension of truth, not just grace. Please hear me in the Spirit. If you are in the spirit, you will realize that grace and truth speak of the same matter. Grace admits to Adam's nature in the flesh and Christ's in our spirits. Occasionally grace highlights God's plan that He wants it to be all Christ and this Adam virus to be done away with. Truth brings all that to light.

In grace, our humanity is tolerated; we are somewhat expected to be flawed and weak in the flesh. However, we are invited to come to the highest point of expressing our divinity in Christ. A dimension of life swallows up sin and death, working against us.

INTRODUCTION INTO MAMMON

Now, before the fall, there was no money. Money came with the loss of glory, namely, life. Let me take you back a little; Zoe life was natural before the fall. Therefore, faith did not need to draw from it (see chapter 9). This is because Bio life came as a result of sin. What is bio life? It is death itself taking quality time to be completed in the body through sin. Biology is the study of mortality, and Zoelogy is the study of immortality. When you study biology at school, you must cry and say, "Alas, Lord, we have fallen short of your glory!" There is nothing called biology. It's heresy according to God's standards. It's a hoax. "I speak as a fool."

There is no life except God's life; all else is death in disguise, and there's no such thing as human life. There's only divine life; all human life is death working through sin; Adam, my friend, is death itself. Jesus wouldn't die to give us life if we were living and if there's only one life. All else is death or dying.

Now, we come to the issue of money. Just as biology is an apostate doctrine, commerce came through sin and death. Adam is death, and

Mammon operates through the power of death. Look at everything you've bought with money. There's not even one thing you bought with money that does not have an expiry date. Even the Bible you bought will perish. It's only the Word it carries that will live on forever. One can hypothetically say that money is the mark of the beast or the beast itself. This is because, like the mark, no one can buy or sell in this world without money. Yet the scriptures are clear that it is possible to buy and sell without money (Isaiah 55:1-3)

If there's a level where people live abundant lives without money, then money must not be the original plan of God. Another form of currency must have been used before money came along. Isaiah clearly says there's nothing for free, but there is a currency we can use in exchange for material things here on earth.

According to the Great Tribulation theory, this beast or Anti-Christ called death ruled for seven years. This is symbolic of the seven thousand years of Adam's rule on earth. Money, too, is 6013 years old according to dispensationalist years. So, you see, friends, money is a very recent commodity. Adam must have used a different bank account than we know - a different currency.

THE CURRENCY OF LIFE

Read Revelation 22: 1-5

From this revelation, we learn what the Eden economy looked like. A river, here, is symbolic of currency, or let me say it is currency. I know that some will fill much safer if I do not apply allegory in this regard; however, I mean no harm to the prophecy the Lord showed John. I will prove that a river is a currency symbol, a flow.

Now, other than the general understanding of what currency is, currency is anything that sustains or supplies a particular system. It is the push or force that regulates the direction by which movement, progress, and development is given at a given sphere or realm. A river is a currency behind water. When water is forcefully pushed towards a given direction against all odds, it is called a river or current. Unlike the waves of the sea, they are pushed by the wind in a given direction. The sea does not have currency. A river is not pushed by the direction of the wind, but rather it forcefully pushes the waters even against the direction of the wind. The direction of the river comes mainly from geography than the wind.

Therefore, by studying the river of life, we understand the currency that Adam used in Eden before the fall. This currency is called life. In Zion, there is a river of life, or a financial system called divine life, and after the fall, another river called the river of death was introduced to water the garden. Instead of watering it, it destroyed it. The world as we know it was not formerly like this; it was perfect because it was run by a perfect economic system called divinity.

Many people know a lot about the river of Babylon called death, but they are clueless about the river of life. Therefore, it is fitting for me to teach you about kingdom economics and how to get back to that river of life and use it to run things on earth. Let us take a close look at the river of life.

> It is a pure currency that is not contaminated by sin and flesh and cannot be penetrated by the devil.

> It is a transparent system. It is without fraud and shadiness.

> It flows from the throne. God has established His throne and kingdom using divinity.

> It is 100% free of recession, limitations, and poverty (they shall hunger no more. Sound familiar?)

> Its waters are for healing. When mammon finally collapses, this economy shall heal the nations.

> It is curse free.

> Here we shall experience all of God

> The truth of God shall remove all confusion. There shall be
no more darkness.

Therefore, this battle is not about buying and selling versus giving
and receiving. It is about death versus life. Please understand that death is
not the opposite of life but rather the absence of it. We call Zoe light, and
Bio (death disguising itself as life) is what we call darkness. Therefore,
the kingdom of darkness is the bio kingdom which operates and depends
on how much money one has. The kingdom of light, on the other hand,
is the Zoe kingdom which operates and depends on the life of God to
supply all things, and hence we give away mammon to those who belong
to the bio kingdom so that we demonstrate to them the love of God and
win them to our kingdom.

Understand me, both kingdoms may use the same paper called
money and the same bank, but the sources are not the same. The source
of worldly people is death, and death operates through this paper called
money. On the other hand, we can live without money because all things
are provided in divinity. However, we buy and pay in order not "to offend
them."

One can even say that the beast in Revelation 13 is death (or bio life),
and the mark of the beast is worldly economics. Money is the motivation
behind everything you see today and something even behind some big
ministries. People's foreheads and right hands have an unseen tattoo and
idol called Mammon. However, the real idol is death, not money; even
Satan is not greater than death. Satan is one of the angels of death.
Without death's approval and power, Satan is powerless. He operates
through the power of death.

By the rivers of Babylon, there we sat down, yea, we wept, when we
remembered Zion (Psa 137:1)

The scripture indicates that another river or currency operates in Babylon. Secondary, we see that the church can be deported to Babylon and be familiarized with a different river. This means that the positions called Sion and the church are numerically different. Yes, the church is Zion; however Zion is more of a place than a people. The church becomes Zion when she is positioned there. In this case, the church was in Babylon, and according to Psalms, she wept by the Spirit when she remembered the river of life.

HOW TO COME BACK TO ZION?

How do we build our ministries using the rivers of life? When God first revealed that He was shifting the church from prosperity to divinity. I struggled to absorb the part where He said I could live free of charge without spending money on anything.

Even you can agree that money is the answer for everything. But the Lord told me that money answers all things pertaining to bio life (meaning things that perish). He told me that in the beginning, it was not so. In the beginning, all things were eternal, and nothing perished.

Once we return to the river of life, death shall be no more. Mammon, too shall be no more. These things are possible here on earth.

The first step is the Word of faith. Faith is the key to operating at the level of life. In the next chapter, we will explore the Word of faith and how it brings us to the Word of life.

CHAPTER 6

MOVING FROM THE WORD OF FAITH INTO THE WORD OF LIFE

2 Corinthians 4:13, 14; John 6:63
Some may see this transition as unnecessary, but I will show you just how necessary it is. Earlier I said that faith is the key to moving from depending on mammon to divine life. Faith is one of the great pillars of the kingdom, having hope and love superior to it.

Love is the greatest and is shown to be numerically separate from faith. Though faith is powerful, and all things are possible through it, the reality is that all things are possible through love, not faith. Through faith, we tap into the life of God more like what data bundles are to the internet. The bundles help me to surf the net depending on how much I have. For example, I can download some items or watch videos on YouTube if I have one gigabyte.

Everything is possible within the measure of faith one possesses. That is what the Word of faith is all about. Love, on the other hand, does not help us tap into God's life but is God's life. Therefore, we come to the Word of life when we come to love.

Hence, love is the greatest commandment in the Bible. Faith is the data bundle, but love is the internet. People use faith to surf the net, which is divine life. However, when you walk in love, you become the net (supplier, source), and people use their modems and faith to draw life from you (that is if you were God or His son).

Jesus used this format to operate one earth. However, this format is not supported by many programs on earth. Even many churches would rather use faith to tap into God's life than to become life. Now, let me remove the element of confusion: faith is for receiving God, but we become what makes up God through love, His life.

In the above scriptures, we see that Paul teaches the Corinthians about the Word of faith. "We believe, and therefore we speak." That is the slogan of the Word of faith or the Word of Faith movement. It says I must first activate my faith by listening to the Word and then apply it by speaking. This is a powerful life because it introduces us to the supernatural. Through faith, I can experience God's power, presence, and life working in and through me. However, I remain human, still having infirmities in the flesh. This means I and the word I speak are not yet one. Love makes us one with the Word.

Jesus did not use this model. He operated by the Word of life. "We become, and therefore we speak." This should have been the slogan of Paul. We are shifting from the Word of faith to the Word of life.

TOGETHER WITH THIS SHIFT, WE WILL TRANSITION FROM DIVINE HEALING OR HEALTH INTO DIVINE LIFE

Please note that when Jesus healed the sick, He didn't use the prayer of faith, but out of His abundance, He released life. The people received what He was and is by faith, which is life.

This is the life He came to give us. And this life was supposed to become in us the bank or safe by which we redeem all things. Brethren, Christ did not become sick because God healed Him or because He was healthy, but there was no sin or death in His body. He was the source of life. It would be impossible for Him to be sick.

I know that some of you would rather think that God anointed him. Maybe whenever He went to the mountain, He prayed, "Father, I need more of your anointing," like we always do. Oh, no friends, the anointing must be given because of weakness but in Him was no weakness. The Spirit rested on Him not to anoint Him but to glorify Him.

Remember in the garden of Gethsemane when Jesus prayed, wishing the cup would pass before He drank it? At that time, Christ knew He would have to voluntarily receive pain, meaning He was not subject to pain. People could beat Him, and nothing would come out of His flesh had He desired so. This makes His sacrifice even greater because life's source and author became voluntarily enslaved by weakness, sickness, pain, and death. However, the Father did not allow Him to see decay.

He did all that to make us like Him. This means that because now we have His life through Holy Communion with Him, we sin, get sick, feel pain, and even die due to the flesh, there stands a promise of immortality and incorruption for the sons of God. The anointing, friends, does not remove weakness but cry within us for perfection. It is the glory that is a life that makes us perfect. When we fully walk in love, we become eligible for the life God promises.

Read Matthew 5:44-48

We cannot be perfected in life until we are made perfect in love. In this present time, we are being perfected in our love walk. This seemingly simple concept of love is the key to real power and glory.

This is ironic because the love subject, the theme of the Christian faith, is why Pan-Africanists and African Spiritualists hate Christianity. They believe that the whites used the disguise of Christian theology to enslave and colonize Africans. This, of course, is a naïve position about what Christianity stands for and love itself.

A Christianity that is solely based on military weakness and peace as a sign of love is stupid. Therefore, it stands to reason that Africans were given a knockoff version of Christianity. This is not what I am talking about. I am not talking about being weak, gullible, and wrongly applying forgiveness were economic and political reparations are needed.

Africa can be smart and strong militarily and economically and be loving and forgiving. Love is not supposed to be weak and gullible. Africa should not be the dumping place of the world or a victim of imperial bullying in the name of love. This is false love; it is slavery masquerading as love and peace.

Therefore, we are perfected in love. In love, we experience the one true God and His power. This tremendous power that emanates from love causes us to access this life God promises. This life allows us to operate from a higher currency. In other words, God gives us all we ask of Him because our motives are pure, like the river in Revelation 22.

TOGETHER WITH THIS SHIFT, THE CHURCH WILL MOVE FROM DEBT CANCELATION TO ALL THINGS BEING FREE

During the Word of Faith Movement, I learned that we could buy all things cash and owe no man. Men like Dr. Oyedepo have mastered this dimension. However, as powerful as this is, I also learned that I could have everything in the Word of Life without buying them. I used to be puzzled by this revelation. How can I own a 1-billion-rand property without paying a cent? God revealed to me that in this dimension of life, all things are given freely, and mammon becomes useless.

In other words, it matters not whether you are financially rich or poor; nothing can keep you from living the life you trust God for. This life can be accessed by those with no money in the bank.

I've seen this at work in my life by the small things, but I struggled to realize that such levels are possible. God showed me that I must possess such levels in my spirit to activate them and not just confess them. This is what we call divinity. It is way greater than prosperity.

When Adam was in the glory, he only managed what was provided. If anything was hypothetically lacking, he spoke words of life, and the thing became. Jesus also used the same word of life to run His ministry on earth.

Read John 6:5-6

The level of divinity is also a level of divine knowledge. This will be tough to explain. Looking at the gifts of the Spirit, we see how revelation operates. It is a torch of the Spirit, and the revelation gifts (prophecy included) are torchbearers on earth to maintain the light of God in these dark times.

These torchbearers are not the light; hence they must be tested by the light. Christ did not use these torchbearers when He asked Philip the question. He was not being prophetic though people called Him a prophet. However, He used His divine life as light. Remember John 1:4, **"in Him was life; and the life was the light of men."** In this dimension, there is perfect knowledge. We do not see in part like in the prophetic.

Jesus was neither a prophet nor an apostle (He is the Apostle). He is the Son of God who lived, died and rose to bring many sons to the same glory of life which He demonstrated when He was on earth.

Now, let's hypothetically say that when John says, "He knew what to do," the thing He knew to do He never did because Andrew interrupted when he brought the boy with the bread. Let's say Jesus knew that too, but He was going to do something else to feed the people had Andrew not shown up (something like causing bread to appear out of nowhere). What was Jesus going to do? Oh boy! I love this! Jesus was never out of ideas when He was faced with a situation.

I laugh now when I think back, wandering the streets of Hammanskraal, lost in my heart because I had no money to do anything I needed to do. The Lord said, *"Your problem is not money, but your biggest problem is that you are clueless."* He was right, I had no idea what I was doing. I was willing to try anything anywhere to be able to pay the bills; I was stressed.

My life had never been in such a mess. Everything I learned from books and schools was not working for me. I knew in my heart that divine sonship was the answer, but I was lazy and fearful. What if this never worked? Can a man become a life-bearer? But that was my only answer.

You cannot depend on prophecies all your life. I know this from experience. Now I know that divine knowledge and administration are key. Jesus knew what to do, do you? People run from one meeting to another, trying to get direction, but Jesus had all the answers within Him. So, friends, believe me; to run around "trying" to start a ministry or a business might get you hurt. Sit down until you know that you know what to do.

I know that everything that God showed me in all my writings is the key to my success. I know that money is not my answer, but divine life is. My pastor, you can run a successful ministry without a single sponsorship. Yes, you can, but the secret is divinity. The word of life is what you need.

WELCOME TO THE WORD OF LIFE
Galatians 4:1-7; John 5:39

What I'm about to say may contradict some things you learned and may also destroy a few demons in the process. The scriptures are good and have the breath of God, but they are not Christ and, therefore, have no eternal life - Christ does. Knowing this will liberate you, my friend, because there are many theologians and people who thoroughly search the scriptures, but they lack Christ and therefore do not have this life we are talking about.

When we come to Christ, do we do away with the scriptures? God forbid! They testify about Christ. Now, Paul says that the Old Testament church was a slave yet an heir of God's promises. While being a babe, there was a need for tutors, viz., the Law and the Prophets until God appointed to give us eternal life. The tutors testified about life, but they did not carry it or Him. Finally, life came, but people still concentrated on the Law and the prophets instead of believing them and coming to Christ.

The same is true about the word of life today. The scriptures do not carry the word of life, but they carry the word of faith. Our relationship with Christ through the Spirit of holiness carries the word of life. We read the scriptures to believe, but we come to Christ to become. Friends, it is not what you believe that matters, "even demons believe and tremble." It is what you become. You can believe in prosperity, but until you become prosperous in your heart, you cannot prosper [whether you believe in my teaching or not].

Believe me, brethren, Kenneth E. Hagin became in his heart what he believed before it manifested. He didn't have enough words to explain it. If he did not become, then he was plain occultic; that goes for all God's generals. Why do you think the scripture says, "faith works through love?" What you have become causes what you believe in coming to pass.

"And all these, having obtained a good testimony through faith, did not receive the promise" (Heb 11:39).

I want to use this scripture verse to illustrate why people do not receive most of the time. Hermeneutically they did not receive because

God wanted to include us. That is in line with eschatology. However, in most cases, people fail to receive the promise even though they believe because of failure to become.

They believe the Word, but they fail to become the Word. Hence, they do not have what it takes to fully walk in God's promises. The word of life flows straight from our hearts when we are now filled with the word of faith. When the scriptures are alive in us until we are called the Lord's epistles, then life will come out of us, and nothing shall be impossible.

This means I cannot go and stop a funeral just because I believe God can raise the dead. It is not your faith that raises the dead but the deposit of life within you. Do not go for the anointing only but go for the glory - go for eternal life.

THE MISTAKE WE MAKE ABOUT FAITH

There is an error that I wish to rectify here: one can confess things, and then those things will appear. This is not necessarily Biblical faith; it might be New Age faith. True Biblical faith is not an intention or decision but an impartation.

Faith is imparted to us through the hearing of the Word of God. The scriptures say, "it comes." We intentionally apply ourselves to hearing and obeying the Word, and then faith comes. When faith has come, you will know that now you are operating in faith.

In other words, when we pray, fast, and study the Word, we do so to get to faith. Once we get to faith, things begin to happen. Do nothing until you are in faith. This means that faith is not a decision or feeling but a place you get to. Faith is a spirit that comes upon you, an anointing that helps you make things happen. Therefore, one does not always have faith. Hence, we build our faith through praying in the Holy Ghost.

If I was in faith yesterday when a miracle happened, it does not mean I will be in faith today for more miracles to occur. I need to get into faith today for today's miracle. This is the major difference between the word of faith and life. In faith, we must always be in its realm to see miracles, whereas in love, the power flows because of who we are, not what we confess.

During the Word of Faith era, there was too much emphasis on confessing Bible verses to receive. Many people we fooled into thinking a bunch of confessions was enough to make them successful. The newsflash is a long process of becoming one with the Word before seeing the manifestation. A verbal denial of your situation won't cut.

CHAPTER 7

RACING WITH HORSES - A PROPHETIC KEY FOR YOUR SUCCESS

"**I**f you have run with the footmen, and they have wearied you, how can you contend with horses? And *if* in the land of peace, *In which* you trusted, *they wearied you,* Then how will you do in the floodplain of the Jordan?" (Jer 12:5)

I love the subject of prophetic keys; hence, I include it in almost all my writings because my heart goes out to God's children who love and fear God but lack the proper keys to advance their own lives. The more I study the prophetic, the more I understand that it is God's emergency response to the cries of His people.

If only people knew how to use prophetic keys, they would win in business and life. In this chapter, we will look at the subject of supernatural speed. Supernatural speed allows you to compete with the best in business or other areas of life without having the proper help or equipment they have.

To race with horses is to operate with a high speed of success and effectiveness without any support or resources. This book is necessary for black entrepreneurs because we do not have the kind of help and systemic privilege that white people have. Learning the prophetic and the supernatural is a better way of getting ahead, even though you might not be as connected as others.

Racing with horses is a blueprint that gives people with a poor background the ability to level the Plainfield using prophetic tools. I would love to call myself a prophetic connoisseur because of my poor background. Poverty taught me how to depend on God fully. This made me master the God art. I have mastered the art of prayer, fasting, and giving; I know these things work.

I know what the favor of God can do for a man, and how to get out of financial crises through faith. I can testify that racing with horses is possible if you believe and allow yourself to become what God wants for you.

BE CAREFUL OF ENEMIES OF PROGRESS

"Dan shall be a serpent by the way, a viper by the path, that bites the horse's heels so that its rider shall fall backward" (Gen 49:17).

Enemies of progress are serpentine in nature. They can be demonic spirits or real people. Dan was prophesied that he would be a serpent that bites the heels of a horse so that the rider falls backward. Dan was an enemy of someone's progress.

A horse is anything God has blessed you with that helps you go forward. This can be your finances, business, ministry etc. the serpent bites the horse so that you fall. The serpent's job is to either stop you or slow you down.

It is important to discern an enemy of progress in your life. Usually, an enemy of progress has one of the following serpentine spirits possessing them:

1. Leviathan. This is a spirit of witchcraft.
2. Mermaid. This is a spirit of occult practices.
3. Python. This is a spirit of divination.
4. Viper. This is a spirit of false brethren.
5. Asp. This is a spirit of deceit.
6. Cobra. This is a spirit of pride.
7. Family serpent. This is a familiar spirit.

Some marine spirit usually possesses enemies of progress. It is important to discern if someone is possessed by these demonic spirits and know how to deal with them.

The prophetic gives the believer an advantage in the business world because prophetic people have the proceeding word of God in them. The proceeding word is for life. When we constantly draw from the proceeding word of God, we allow the river of life to water our everyday lives continuously.

Prophetic ministry speaks for those who cannot speak for themselves; it fights for those who cannot fight for themselves. It gives the disenfranchised a fighting chance by boosting their economic speed supernaturally. Even though I might come from generations of pain and poverty through the prophetic, I can rise and compete with leading men and women in their respective fields, whether in medicine, education, or business.

Therefore, prophetic people are not victims of past misfortunes caused by the atrocities committed on our forefathers. Prophetic people do not need your pity and your handouts. They can rise on their own by walking in divinity.

Prophetic thinkers (Ehuds) can manipulate the system and find themselves ahead of those who had initially used systemic privilege to progress in life. Speaking of the African nations and the Diaspora, I learned that the prophetic is our heritage. This means prophesying or seeing in the spirit is in our blood. We did not begin to operate in the supernatural when we came to Christ.

Christ showed us how to operate the godly way, but we were already developed in interpreting spiritual signs and language. Therefore, I am not here to say something new but to emphasize that what you have believed was always the correct key to your success.

Don't miss out!

Visit the website below and you can sign up to receive emails whenever Nicholas Dlamini publishes a new book. There's no charge and no obligation.

https://books2read.com/r/B-A-NKQAB-WMSWC

BOOKS2READ

Connecting independent readers to independent writers.

Did you love *Kingdom Commerce*? Then you should read *How To Operate In Secular Babylon*[1] by Nicholas Dlamini!

The greatest expression of the New Testament church, as outlined in the book of Ephesians, is the army. I believe the army dimension is higher than the bride, the body, or the city. The army allows us to see the fulfillment of God's promises to His bride.

This book is about taking back what the enemy has stolen and returning to Zion. For that to happen, we need believers trained in covert operations. We need people that know how to operate in secular Babylon.

This manuscript is about raising prophetic people who can infiltrate the secular world for the kingdom's sake. Kingdom people are not only

---

1. https://books2read.com/u/boBoPA

2. https://books2read.com/u/boBoPA

those who sing Christian songs and speak in tongues, but it is people who know how to represent the kingdom in the world.

About the Author

Nicholas Dlamini is an apostolic and prophetic preacher of the gospel. He is senior pastor and founder of Dabar Word Centre at Ludzeludze in the kingdom of ESwatini. He runs a weekly podast on WhatsApp titled "Prophetic Podcast". The rest of his teachings can be found on his YouTube channels titled: intense word sessions with Nicholas Dlamini and Dabar Word Centre.